Jingle Time

Rhymes and songs for early years learning

Christine Macintyre

with music by Mike Carter

David Fulton Publishers
London

David Fulton Publishers Ltd
The Chiswick Centre, 414 Chiswick High Road, London W4 5TF

www.fultonpublishers.co.uk

David Fulton Publishers is a division of Granada Learning Limited, part of the Granada Media Group

First published in Great Britain in 2003 by David Fulton Publishers
10 9 8 7 6 5 4 3 2 1

Copyright © 2003 Christine Macintyre (text); Mike Carter (music)

British Library Cataloguing in Publication Data
A catalogue record for this book is available from the British Library.

ISBN 1-84312-027-5

Cover design by Phil Barker
Illustrations by Jane Bottomley
Designed and typeset by Kenneth Burnley, Wirral, Cheshire
Printed and bound in Great Britain by Thanet Press Limited, Margate, Kent

Contents

Acknowledgements

A huge 'thank you' to all those who have helped to prepare the materials for this book. First, to the teachers and children who have tried the jingles and made many useful suggestions as to how they could be used, both in the hall and in the classroom. Special thanks to Rhona Lees at Longniddry Primary, Anne Revels at Tweedbank in the Scottish Borders and to Nichola Jones from Bridgend in Wales.

Mike Carter wrote the music, so a big vote of thanks goes to him for adding to the fun.

The biggest thank you of all, of course, goes to the children who drew the lovely illustrations and decorated their classrooms with ideas springing from the jingles. Some even became models for the photographs! My thanks go to them all.

Note on the tunes

The tunes in this book are designed for young pupils to sing and have simple piano (or keyboard) accompaniments. Appropriate guitar chords are listed underneath and may replace or augment the piano accompaniments. There are also suggestions for pupils to help accompany the songs using common percussion instruments.

The songs can also be used to help teach aspects of music. For example, there are songs in common, waltz time and 6/8 time. Songs such as 'The Kindly Giant' have a typical A - B - A - C form. The accompaniments also reflect several different musical styles, for example, 'Rainy Days' uses a typical Mozartian style. Discussion about the nature of each song can lead to greater awareness of musical features such as timbre.

Several songs, for example 'Special Day', encourage some degree of personalising while others prompt actions such as clapping, e.g. 'Dancing Hands'. However, we hope that you will experiment and suggest that pupils clap and join in with the songs in several ways. In this way they may gain a better sense of the difference between pulse (the regular beat) and rhythm (a beat pattern for the song).

Introduction

This book provides a dip-in selection of rhymes and jingles which can be used as a stimulus for many kinds of learning. The ideas and themes are based on those which are often used in the early years' classrooms with children aged 4–8 or so. The most obvious use for the jingles is that the children listen and act out the storylines. They can take a variety of parts either individually or in groups. They love being the giant who tosses boulders down the mountainside or the sailors who row away to find adventure or the clown who is sad when he must leave the circus. In this way, they learn about different kinds of lives and, through discussing how these 'people' must feel, they begin to realise that others have hopes and dreams and sad times too. Perhaps they might relate some of these experiences to their own world and be more accepting of other people's views?

Some of the rhymes help the children learn things they need to know, for example, the days of the week, the kinds of birds which visit gardens, even the kinds of weather which can be expected in different seasons. The rhyme makes it easy for children to learn and remember. The short jingles can be learned through daily repetition and, in the longer ones, groups of children can work on different verses and then put them all back together again. Perhaps this could build into a kind of 'performance' for school assemblies or parents' evenings? Some of the rhymes are useful in that they give brief movement breaks which can interspace with other aspects of learning which need the children to be still for rather a long time. These are usually very popular and teachers claim there is increased attention after the break!

Learning through rhyme and rhythm helps all kinds of development, e.g. language becomes more fluid and vocabulary can be readily extended, while everyone remembers 'sums' more easily if rhythmic jingles are part of learning! In fact, current thinking about dyslexia is suggesting that there is a positive link between exposure to rhythm and later reading skills. On top of that, and very importantly, children learn to move in an expressive way as they act out the ideas and develop scenarios of their own. In expressive movement like this, the children have only to cope with their own bodies rather than having to control apparatus such as a bat and a ball or deal with quite difficult skills such as climbing and jumping which could be required in a gymnastics lesson. So there are fewer 'outside' demands and the children are freed to be imaginative and expressive at whatever level of complexity they choose.

Ideas for development are given in the Teacher's Notes which accompany each jingle, but of course these are only suggestions and the children may well have their own ideas about what they would like to do. They can act them out and/or sing them, draw their favourite parts or write stories of their own based on the ideas contained in them. The children may well enjoy developing the storyline in quite a different way from the one that is suggested here.

Recalling events in the correct order helps sequencing. All the ideas can be developed through group or class discussions. Music is provided for most of the jingles so that the children can sing-along or play percussion. The centre pages of the book have colour illustrations for four of the jingles: the clown, the pirate, the puppet and the spider. These pages can be pulled out, so that you can cut out and laminate the characters, and make them into stick puppets. These can then be used in a range of activities and role plays. This gives another way to stimulate and reinforce the learning that is going on. The most important thing is that the children – and their teachers – enjoy these teaching and learning experiences: I hope they do! The 'early learning goals' in the New Framework for Early Years' Education, Child Care and Play work and the criteria in the Curriculum 3–8 documents have been carefully considered in producing this book, which sets out fun ways of achieving them all.

Jingle 1: **The Kindly Giant**

Drum:

Jingle 1: **The Kindly Giant**

1. There are giant footprints on the path outside,
   a right one and a left one
   make one great big stride.
   What kind of size do you think that giant might be?
   Perhaps he'll be taller
   than the tallest tree!

   - **look around**
   - **move right foot, then left foot**
   - **giant step**
   - **scratch head**
   - **stretch up with hands in air**

2. But where is the giant? Where on earth is he?
   I'm going to hide
   where he can't see me!
   Is he an ogre with eyes so harsh and grey?
   If by chance he looks like that
   we'll all run away!

   - **look around**
   - **crouch down**
   - **cover eyes**
   - **make ugly face**

   - **pretend to run**

3. Listen hard, I hear him coming down the lane.
   Let's peep out and see him
   then we'll hide again,
   Did you see his big red nose and his merry twinkling eyes?
   I'm sure he is a kindly giant;
   what a nice surprise!

   - **hand to ear**
   - **peep**
   - **crouch again**
   - **point to nose and eyes**
   - **smile**
   - **make surprised face**

4. He's sitting in our garden saying, 'Please come and play,
   I love to see young children,
   they brighten up my day.'
   And so we'll run to him and climb upon his knee
   and ask him to tell us all
   his history!

   - **sit down and beckon**

   - **smile**
   - **run and pretend to climb**

5. 'When I was a little boy,' our kindly giant said,
   'I lived up in the mountains
   where the sky is red.
   I tossed huge boulders down the mountainside
   and swam the lakes
   and made towns shake
   and travelled far and wide.

   - **low hand**
   - **pretend to draw mountains**

   - **pretend to toss boulders**
   - **swim**
   - **shake**

6. 'But now I'm older, it hurts me to see,
   how lots of little children
   are afraid of me.
   So now I keep smiling and do my best to show
   that though I'm big, I'm just a kid at heart
   you know.'

   - **holding walking stick**

   - **cowering**
   - **smile**

   - **hand on heart**

The Kindly Giant: *Teacher's Notes*

This rhyme holds lots of possibilities for both movement and drama. The children can either act out the story individually as it unfolds – there are suggestions written alongside – or one child can be the narrator, one the giant and the others the village children who are fearful and then relieved when they discover the giant is a friendly one! Children love adding actions to this rhyme. Although it is quite long, there are lots of actions and movements to keep them interested.

The children can

- discuss what a giant looks like;
- gather descriptive words, e.g. huge, frightening, friendly;
- choose a scene to draw – see children's examples;
- discuss how a giant feels, e.g. lonely, angry, or sad when the children won't play (this could lead to discussions about when they feel sad or angry or how they feel when they are left out of playground games);
- draw a friendly giant or an angry giant;
- discuss what a giant might wear e.g. big, clumpy boots;
- begin to gather pairs of opposites:

big	small
enormous	tiny
friendly	frightening
merry	sad
gentle	harsh, etc.

- pick out the action words and practise these, e.g. peep, stare, hide, run away, shaking, climbing.

Discussion

At the start, the children probably decide that a giant is a fierce, frightening character and if they met him they would be sure to run and hide. However, he turns out to be lonely and friendly. The children might discuss how they could tell (e.g. what did the giant look like, what kinds of things did he do to give them clues about his character?). This could lead to children making different facial expressions and their partner deciding what emotion they were trying to display – this activity would be helpful for children who find reading non-verbal cues difficult – and it's fun to try showing different characteristics.

The children will be used to having smiley faces. They might like to try drawing frightened, hurt, grumpy, sad and angry faces too (see non-smiley faces on p. 7). This helps them recognise emotions, and discussions about the best kind of response, e.g. 'What would you do if you met someone grumpy?' and 'How do you look when you feel cross? What do others do then?' could be useful follow-on questions which should help develop empathy and altruism.

I'm sticking my head out of the
chimney. The giant is going to
knock my house down with the
boulder.

The giant is tossing the boulder. I'm hiding in the tree.

We are all hiding from
the giant.

The giant threw boulders.

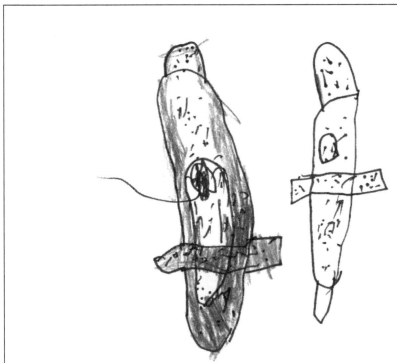

I was hiding and I saw some footprints and I wanted to have a look for a giant.

HAPPY   SAD

HURT   ANGRY

FRIGHTENED   MAKE A FACE HERE

Jingle 2: **Good Morning and Goodbye**

In the morning

Jingle 2: **Good Morning and Goodbye**

1. Good morning, good morning.
   It's (Mon)day today.
   We're sitting so nicely
   and what do we say?

2. Good morning to everyone
   everyone here.
   We'll have lots of fun
   so let's stand up and cheer!

3. We'll play with all our friends
   But we'll work so hard too.
   We'll write and we'll paint
   and there's lots more to do!

4. So now we'll get started
   enjoying our day.
   Come everyone, join in
   and let's be away!

Do not over-emphasise the 'oom-pa-pa' nature of this song but try 'shake, tap, tap' with a tambourine.

Recorder descant

Jingle 2: **Good Morning and Goodbye**

At home time

Jingle 2: **Good Morning and Goodbye**

1. Goodbye to everyone.
   What do we say?
   We'll see you tomorrow,
   another good day.

2. Go safely, safely,
   mind how you go.
   We'll see you tomorrow,
   that's (*Tues*)day, you know!

Chime bars

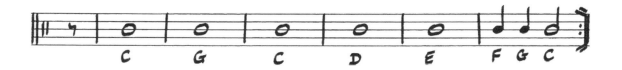

C   G   C   D   E   F G C

11

Good Morning and Goodbye: *Teacher's Notes*

These two jingles can be used to begin and end the day. They provide a welcome to the children in the morning and a caring message when it's time to go home. They engender a sense of togetherness and of everyone being valued in the class.

They also do the following:

- provide a positive input – everyone welcoming and smiling to everyone else;
- help everyone to feel involved from the start of the day;
- provide signals that everyone is ready;
- help everyone settle, ready for whatever comes next;
- provide a secure routine – the children know what's coming and they know they are ready to cope.

Apart from this, of course, the jingle helps the children learn the names of the days of the week and their sequence. If the jingle is enlarged on the photocopier, one child each day can affix the names of the days (written on card) with blu-tac in the appropriate place. The rhyme also helps them remember what lessons are in the pipeline for that day. Other names can be substituted for writing and painting if they are not part of a particular day.

One class of eight-year-olds took this idea a step further and built their own class timetable by illustrating paper plates which could be changed around. The teacher wrote the break times and lunch-time cards. Gradually, the children had enough plates to cover the curriculum and then they could interchange them daily. One child who had dyspraxia, and so had great difficulty with

Photo 1: Children make their own timetable to help planning and organisation.

remembering what came next in the daily routine, was one of a group who had the responsibility of checking with the teacher and then putting the day's timetable in place. This was a 'hidden' strategy to give a visual reminder and thus reduce the stress for the children who found remembering difficult.

Jingle 3: **Rainbows**

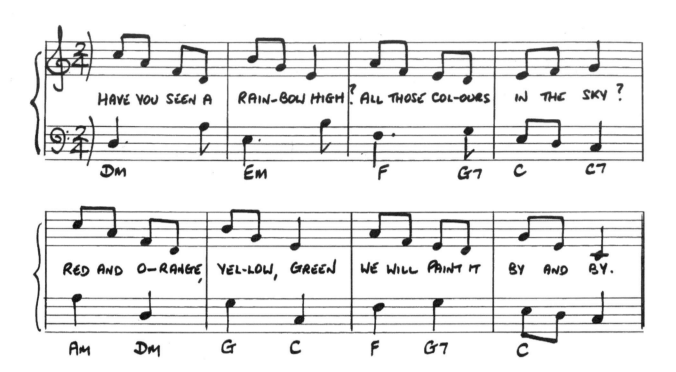

Jingle 3: **Rainbows**

1. Have you seen a rainbow high?
   All those colours in the sky?
   Red and orange, yellow, green
   We will paint it by and by.

2. Can you see the blue shows now,
   hiding just a line below?
   Underneath the blue arc there
   sits the colour indigo.

3. Violet is the final one,
   and another gentle hue.
   It is time to choose your best
   then for you to paint it too.

Use a rain-maker or tubular bells at the beginning of each line of verse.

Rainbows: *Teacher's Notes*

This rhyme is not particularly suitable for actions, but it works very well as a listening activity. Read the rhyme through once, then repeat it while the children draw the rainbow, following the instructions. This rhyme has three main aims:

1. The children learn the different colours of the rainbow and, for the older ones, the order in which they come. The children love a mnemonic to help them do this:

   e.g. Run On You Grizzly Bear In Vain.

2. The children learn

   a) spatial concepts, e.g. over/under/through/below/above (and possibly beyond for the older ones);

   b) colour tones, e.g. light/dark; pale/bright; lighter than/darker than; blending; shadows.

3. The children learn to draw the arc of the rainbow. This shows if the children have achieved hand dominance (i.e. that they consistently use a preferred hand). If they can complete the rainbow without changing hands, it shows that they can cross the midline of the body. Some children find this very difficult and if the difficulty persists after age six, when myelination of the axons should be complete, it just *might* be an early indication of a specific learning difficulty such as dyspraxia. This allows early help to be obtained.

   Painting the rainbow, then, needs fine motor skills (to hold and manipulate the paintbrush), hand dominance (to know which hand to use), and the capability to cross the midline of the body. All of these are important skills which need to be developed if the children are to flourish in a practical curriculum.

Jingle 4: **The Pirate Ship**

Drum: 1st beat of each bar.
Cymbal: Beat on: 'Yo, Tally Ho'

1. A Pirate ship, a pirate ship,
   Yo, Tally Ho!
   Sailing o'er the wide blue seas,
   let's watch it go.

   – wave arms above head
   – make wave actions
   – all look through telescope (cardboard tube)

2. And can you hear the pirates cry?
   Yo, Tally Ho!
   Skull and crossbones flying high,
   let's watch it blow.

   – listen
   – wave arms as above
   – cross arms, wave hands

3. They scale the rigging as they shout   – **climbing action**
    Yo, Tally Ho!   – **wave arms**
    Seeing if a ship's about,   – **looking through telescope**
    they'll make it go.

4. They're off to find some rich treasure,   – **digging action**
    Yo, Tally Ho!   – **wave arms**
    Fighting gives them much pleasure.   – **mock fight, no contact**
    It's the life they know.   – **sword-fighting actions**

5. Each has a cutlass in his hand,
    Yo, Tally Ho!   – **wave arms**
    Kept within their cummerbund,   – **replace cutlass in cummerbund**
    ready to go.

6. They make their prisoners walk the plank,   – **careful walking**
    Yo, Tally Ho!   – **wave arms**
    Thinking it's a jolly prank,   – **pirates point to the plank**
    best way they go.   – **pirates hold sides and laugh**

7. But when the coastguards come along,   – **coastguards strut**
    Yo, Tally Ho!   – **wave arms**
    Then they sing a different song,
    hiding below.   – **pirates climb down into hold to hide**

8. The pirates wrap themselves in chains,   – **coastguards wrap chains around pirates**
    Yo, Tally Ho!   – **wave arms**
    Struggling to be free again
    wish they could go.   – **pirates struggle but gradually sink down**

9. No longer can they roam the seas,
    Yo, Tally Ho!   – **wave arms**
    Now good folks go where'er they please,
    that's how they go!   – **others (good folks) 'strut' – shaking hands as they go**

The Pirate Ship: *Teacher's Notes*

Most children love being pirates and dressing up just needs a few eye patches, scarves and belts. Making pirate hats from folded newspapers and pirate cutlasses from cardboard gives lots of practice in folding and cutting out. Life-size draw-arounds can give each child a pirate model to clothe. Discussions about why pirates wore such clothes (bright to frighten off their enemies and raggy because they had so much work on board ship, were suggestions from one group of six-year-olds!).

There are a number of 'new' action phrases in this jingle which usually capture the interest of very young children – scaling the rigging, walking the plank, pulling the cutlass from the cummer-bund, plundering loot! Waving arms in each verse gives repetition (fun) and encourages listening skills. There is also a moral in the story, i.e. that pirates who break the law will be captured and punished for their misdeeds.

Linked Classroom Activities

*   Making draw-around life-size models and dressing them in pirate clothes.
*   Drawing a treasure island – large-scale to allow different features to be added, e.g. cliffs to make landing treacherous, palm trees and coconuts to provide food and shelter, a shallow bay to beach the boat, wood for a fire, a spring for water, a waterfall to make sounds, exotic animals, e.g. snakes and bats, so that hammocks are essential. Caves (large cardboard boxes) hide the treasure which the pirates have stolen.
*   Treasure maps to find the islands.
*   Treasure chests to hold the plunder. The children can make both the chests and the treasure.

Photo 2: Toys from home can be brought to school.

- Necklaces from threading coloured beads or painted scrolls of paper.
- Golden goblets and pieces of gold.
- Rosaries and precious gems of different colours.

If each child makes something to go into the treasure chest, they become totally involved in the story.

The treasure is under the sea. The pirate is looking for it. He is using the treasure map.

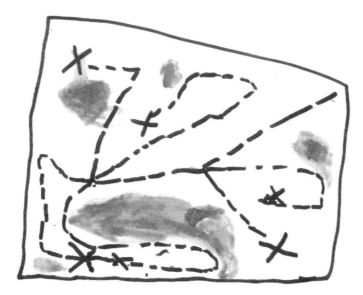

A treasure map, a pirate ship
and a parrot!

The pirate is walking the plank.

This is a pirate and a skull and crossbone.

Jingle 5: **Spin the Brolly**

To emphasise the magical nature of this song, try the following.

Play rain-maker, tubular bells or shaken tambourine whenever the guitar chord is Dm.

Play this rhythm on a small drum or claves:

Beat a cymbal or triangle lightly on the last word of the 2nd and 4th line of each verse.

Jingle 5: **Spin the Brolly**

1. Come under my brolly,
   let's all fly away.
   We'll have an adventure,
   what do you say?

   - holding imaginary brolly up high
   - beckoning to others

   - one questions, others nod

2. Where shall we all go to?
   Who will choose today?
   —— is a good place,
   we'll go straightaway!

   - huddle in a group

   - rush out . . . ready . . .

3. Spin, spin the brolly,
   make it fly up high.
   Then it will make magic
   take us to the sky!

   - spin round (the children are the brolly or they can pretend to hold one)

   - point to sky

4. O'er hilltops and mountains,
   down there is the sea.
   It's lovely just flying,
   glad you're with me?

   - move on toes and then swoop down
   - make wave motion with hand
   - arms wide, running/flying

5. Look yonder, look yonder,
   a polar bear I see.
   He's not soft and cuddly,
   looks fierce to me.

   - looking out
   - waddling or crawling and stretching out

   - begging – growling, waving front paws

6. Out over the icebergs,
   startlingly white.
   See seals and penguins,
   a wonderful sight.

   - waddle like a penguin, hands close to sides; feet out!

7. But it is so chilly
   over this cold land.
   We'll fly to the sunshine,
   there we'll get tanned.

   - shiver; wrap arms around body; stamp feet

   - hands and fingers stretched: fly
   - put on suncream

8. So spin the brolly.
   Make it fly up high.
   And it will make magic,
   take us to the sky!

   - spin round as above

   - point to sky

9. Look down, there are palm trees
   Right around the bay.
   Folk swimming and surfing
   all through the day.

   - standing still, waving fronds

   - swimming – arm action
   - pretend to be on surfboard

10. Some people are jumping
    into the blue sea.
    They're splashing and diving,
    wish it was me!

    - pretend to jump off

    - dive; splashing action

11. Now where shall we go to?   – **fingers on lips**
    Where else shall we roam?   – **questioning look**
    It's all been so lovely
    let's now go home.   – **run to 'home'!**

12. Spin, spin the brolly,   – **spin round**
    say 'It has been grand.   – **call out words loudly**
    But please Mr Brolly
    take us to land.'

13. We're safely at home now,
    stories all to tell.
    And brolly is resting,   – **close brolly and all sit together; yawning then sleeping**
    he's done so well!

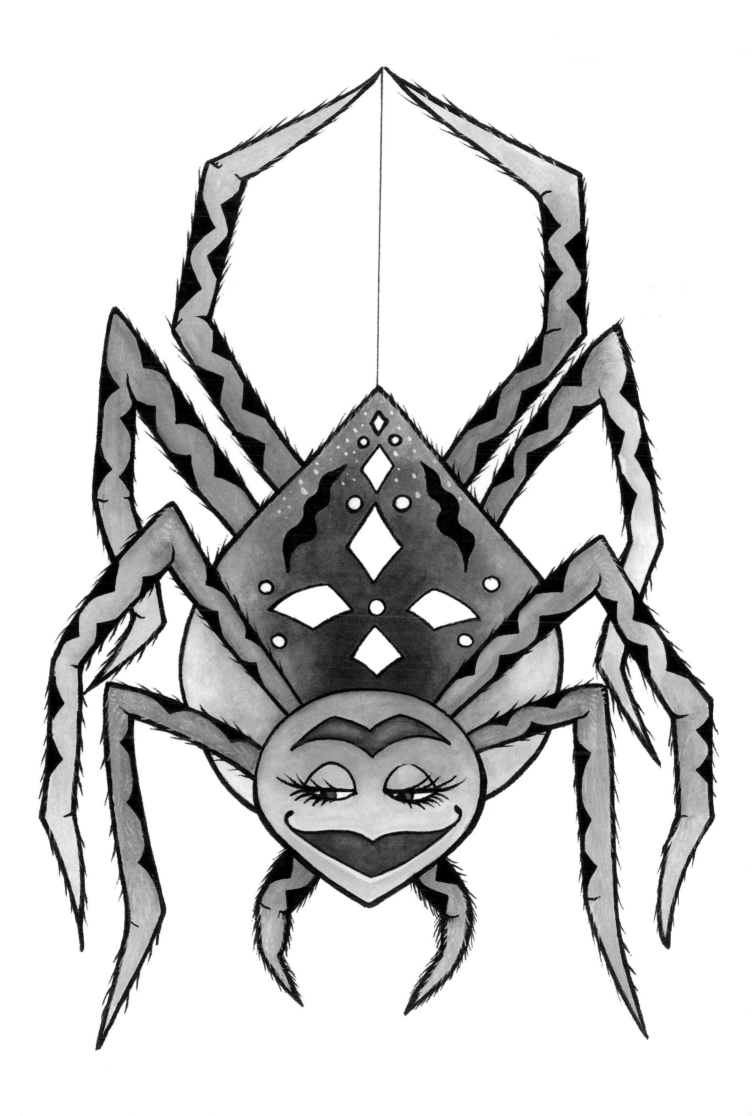

Spin the Brolly: *Teacher's Notes*

This jingle is best for six-, seven- and eight-year-olds. The brolly can either be a child-size one – and one to each group of children is ideal – or the teacher could use a large parasol and stay 'in charge' of the activity. This would be possible with a small class.

Preparatory discussion

The teacher explains that the brolly is magic, just like a magic carpet and that it can take them to far-off lands. Where would they like to go? Perhaps the class could be subdivided so that each child goes to a favourite place. Pictures of exotic, contrasting lands, e.g. the Caribbean beaches or huge icebergs can make the magic journey appeal!

Learning can also be extended if the children bring in toy bears or seals or penguins because then information about the real animals in the real land can be appropriate and will add to the value of the lesson. Questions such as, 'How does a polar bear survive on the ice?', 'Why is a seal such a wonderful swimmer yet so clumsy on land?' or 'Why are there no trees and flowers on the ice?' all help the children's understanding of the natural world.

Photo 3: A huge brolly made in the classroom.

Using the jingle

Groups of children can act out one verse each and then put the whole together or each group can do the whole jingle – travelling from land to land and spinning the brolly when it's time to move on and time to go home.

A little girl is holding on to her umbrella.

I am holding an umbrella.

This is the polar bears and the cracked ice.

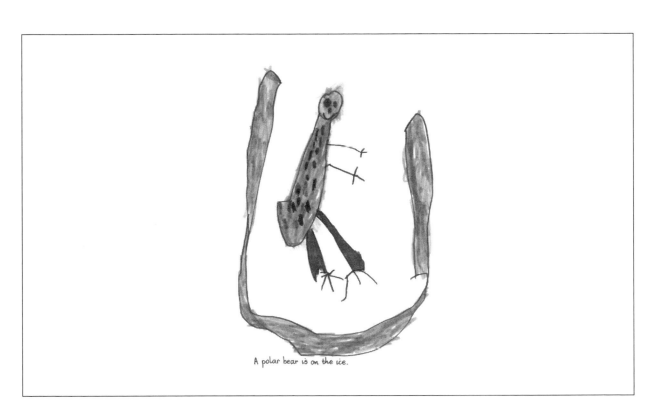

A polar bear is on the ice.

Jingle 6: **Postman Sam**

Jingle 6: **Postman Sam**

1. I am Sam the old Postman,
   and I have lots to do.
   Early in the morning
   I bring the post to you.

2. I've a heavy, bright red bag,
   with packets large and small.
   I know where the people stay,
   I don't get lost at all!

3. I pop letters in your door
   and hope that you will say,
   'Morning Sam', and 'Thanks a lot'
   and 'Have a happy day!'

4. Best of all is summertime,
   when mornings are so bright.
   Harder in the winter when
   there's hardly any light.

5. Ice and snow make walking hard,
   my boots they crunch and slide.
   When big dogs jump out at me
   I wish that I could hide!

6. Still I love my job, you know,
   the only thing I'd be.
   It's so great when children call
   'Is there something for me?'

7. Cards and parcels big and small
   I know that they bring joy.
   I hope there's a special one
   For every girl and boy!

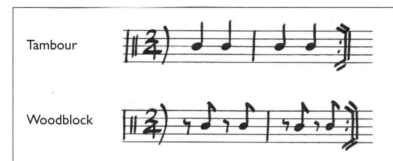

Play a 'C' chime bar on the first word of the first and third lines of each verse and on the last word of each verse.

Postman Sam: *Teacher's Notes*

The idea behind this jingle, i.e. understanding the jobs of 'People who help us', can be expanded to include policemen, firemen, nurses, lollipop ladies, etc. – even teachers!

Discussion points

Would you like to be a postman? Gather 'yes' and 'no' opinions. Try to have the children justify what they say. If, for example, some say they wouldn't like to carry such a heavy bag, then ask them to think of ways they could overcome this! What would be the advantages/disadvantages of, e.g. having a trolley or whatever the children suggest?

If they decide they would like to be a postman, ask 'What kinds of houses would you like to deliver your letters to?' This can open discussions on high-rise flats where there are lots of stairs and houses which have long drives – the postman then has to walk a long way to deliver just one letter! The meanings of the words like Road, Avenue, Crescent, Close, i.e. words which may show the shape and the size of the layout, can be discussed and can provide useful links with early mapping skills.

Details on the letter front

The teacher can prepare or bring in a large-size letter.

Discuss the stamp – what is imprinted on it? Ask the children to gather examples of other used stamps and compare their size and shape and what is written on them. Talk about other stamps which appear on special occasions, e.g. Christmas, a royal event, or anything topical.

Perhaps they would like to know about people who collect stamps for a hobby – and about imperfections in stamps which make them valuable. They will enjoy the difficult word 'philatelist'!

Discuss the franking mark on the letter – why it is there? Very often it partly obliterates the picture. Is there another way?

Look at the positioning of the address and talk about details of the information that is required. Do the children know their own post code? Could they find out?

Parcels

How do they feel when the postman brings a parcel?

The teacher produces a parcel with something rattling inside. Who is it for? (A classroom toy, e.g. Teddy or the Sailor Man or the Lighthouse Keeper or Katie Morag – someone who the children know and has links to other classroom learning perhaps!) What do the children think will be inside? How could they tell without opening the parcel? What clues are there? (The postmark giving the place and the date it was posted, and the weight give clues as to possibilities.) Try to prevent wild guessing by sharing cumulative questions with the children, e.g. Could it be something to wear? rather than, Is it a scarf or a jersey (or whatever)? This helps develop the children's questioning skills. Perhaps the parcel could come from a town where a child's Granny lives? All the details keep the lesson within the children's own experiences and lets it be meaningful for them.

Old-fashioned parcel

It is unlikely that the children will have seen a parcel tied with string. Discuss the knots, the difficulty of untying them and how when things were scarce, people would never have thought of cutting and throwing away the string – they would carefully roll it up to be used again!

Does Postman Sam ever get a letter thanking him for bringing all the letters and parcels? The class can then write letters and send drawings, to say thank you! They could even design stamps. These letters can then can go in the school post box and someone can write a reply.

All sorts of letters can be developed, e.g. a class one to an alien telling him about the school, letters for Mother's Day, letters to ask an old person or a postman to come into class to explain what things were like long ago – before e-mail!

Jingle 7: **Special Person – Special Day**

Jingle 7: **Special Person – Special Day**

1. Someone has a special day?
   It's (*Jonathan*), it's (*Jonathan*).
   He can choose the games we'll play,
   lucky boy today.

2. We'll go into a circle now
   put him in the ring.
   Then he'll choose a special song
   for us all to sing.

3. It is (*Jonathan's*) special day,
   a special boy you see.
   We're his friends, we want to play,
   what will his game be?

4. (*Jonathan*) must make the choice
   and tell us what to play.
   We shall play at ———— now
   he must lead the way.

5. Well done him, well done again,
   what is it we say?
   (*Jonathan's*) a special boy
   on his special day!

Chime bars

Try the following:
- Triangle beat on first beat of each bar.
- Speaking verse 1 and verse 5.
- Additional drum beat:

Special Person – Special Day: *Teacher's Notes*

This is a jingle to boost the self-esteem of children and as such it can complement activities such as circle time and positive reinforcement strategies.

Obviously, birthday children will be chosen on these days so some organisation is needed so that every child has a turn of being special. Some schools pop name tags into balloons and when one is burst the name falls out. This adds to the anticipation and the surprise!

Discussion points

What can all the other children do to make sure that (the child's) day is special?

- Let him or her play
- Be kind
- Be generous in sharing pencils etc.
- Welcome him or her in the morning
- Sit with him or her at lunch, etc.

Discussion

- How do you feel when it's your special day?
- Anxious to come to school? One or two children may not like the extra attention!
- Should we try to make every day special for someone?
- Who really needs a special day? Children overseas who aren't as lucky as the children at this school?
- What could the children at this school do? Sing carols to raise money for a charity; have a sponsored silence; perhaps collect clothes?
- What would it be like if you never ever had anyone telling you were special? Can you draw or write to say thank you to someone at home because they make you feel special? (One child wrote 'I love my Mummy because my Mummy loves me'!)

Looking in the Garden: *Teacher's Notes*

This jingle is to alert children to the variety of wildlife that is around them and to encourage them to be observant.

The children can make lists of creatures they see and bar graphs to note how often they are seen – so this jingle can be linked to early maths.

What can you do to encourage wildlife to come to the garden?' (Is it possible to have a small patch of garden at school if there is none at home?)

Try to engender a sense of wonder, e.g. looking at a butterfly and realising that a whole life cycle happens in such a small creature. Hopefully, this will let the children realise how easily they can be damaged or killed.

Size discussions

What are the smallest and the biggest creatures the children know? Make lists. Note where they live and the kind of habitat which determines their coats, e.g. polar bears, or their body shape, e.g. seals whose smooth, streamlined shape means that they swim well but are ungainly on land. What do they eat? Would they attack people or are they timid?

Lifestyle discussions/habitat

Discussions about the lifestyle of one or two creatures which are seen or unseen can be developed, e.g. the mole who lives underground: its large feet push the earth aside and so help tunnelling; or the squirrel which uses its tail to help balancing. What do these creatures eat?

This can lead into discussion of simple life cycles, e.g. the tadpole/frog cycle, or into giving information about the different creatures, e.g. the good that the worm does by aerating the soil and how it is vegetarian, so little beasts and bugs are spared!

Other discussions

*   What are the good/bad things about having a garden?
*   What would you like to grow?
*   What sorts of conditions help plants to grow? Link to growing cress in the classroom – avocado stones into plants – marigolds which flower easily.
*   What creatures would you hope would visit you?
*   Linked poems, e.g. 'Ladybird, Ladybird' are always enjoyed.

Jingle 8: **Looking in the Garden**

Jingle 8: **Looking in the Garden**

1. Let's look in the garden.
   What do we see?
   A lovely floaty butterfly,
   a zooming, buzzy bee.

2. Caterpillar crawling,
   ever so slow.
   And over there a firefly
   with wings all aglow.

3. On the grass two blackbirds,
   squabbling again.
   And underneath the flowers
   is a tiny jenny wren.

4. Squirrel in the tall tree
   climbing up high.
   And can you see his bushy tail
   and sparkling little eye?

5. Close your eyes and tell me,
   what did you see?
   Remember three small creatures?
   Can you tell them now to me?

CAMERON AGE 5 DREW THE DUCK HE SAW.

Jingle 9: **All at Sea!**

1. I'm a jolly sailor,
   sailing out to sea.
   If you'd like to come along
   Jump aboard with me!

2. Pull the oars so strongly,
   Yo, Heave Ho!
   Now we're out into the waves,
   where shall we all go?

3. Let's sail round that island,
   waves are choppy there.
   Rocks are jaggy round the shore,
   sailors must beware!

4. Over there's a patch of sand,
   Yo, Heave Ho!
   It's a place where we might land,
   come on, now let's go!

5. Jump down in the shallows,
   pull the boat ashore.
   Lots of caves beyond the waves,
   time now to explore!

6. What was on the island?
   Gather round and say,
   treasure, gold or maps so old?
   Now we must away!

7. Climb back in the boat now
   row, row and row.
   Heading homeward happily,
   Yo, Heave ho!

> Try using a rain-maker for the 1st and 2nd line of each verse and a wood block for the 3rd and 4th line of each verse.

All at Sea!: *Teacher's Notes*

This jingle really needs to be acted out in the hall at drama time. The children love to sit in threes, one behind the other and row their boats! It can be fun if boats are made out of equipment in the gym, but this is not really necessary.

The children must get into the boat carefully so as not to capsize it, then row together – this takes some planning to get a rhythm going! (Link with sea shanties!) This is a good opportunity for the teacher to identify children who are wary of others, or who can't follow a common rhythm.

Then when the boat is beached the children have to leap out (jumping over the waves) to haul the boat above the waterline. (Discuss why this would be wise!)

The different groups can then have a pow-wow as to how they are going to explore the island. Discuss what precautions they should take. How will they move as they investigate the unknown territory?

Discussion

The children could discover that their boat has been holed and they will have to spend the night on the island.

- What would they try to find? Food – coconuts? How would they reach them? Fish? How would they catch them? Water – is there a waterfall nearby? Or a spring? Where would they begin to look? Shelter – how would they construct a shelter? What would they use? Fire – why would they need a fire? Warmth and safety. What would they need to make a fire? Should they all set out to gather wood or should they make a plan?
- What could they do to ensure that no-one gets lost?
- How can they let people at home know they are marooned?
- Perhaps they would like to write letters to put in a bottle?
- If they were setting out again what precautions would they take? This could link to always letting people at home know where they were.

Jingle 10: **Dancing Hands**

1. Let's clap two hands together,
   one, two and three.
   Listen to the sound they make,
   clap them hard and see!

2. Now clasp these hands together,
   hold very still.
   Then begin to clap again,
   do a little twirl!

Try clapping

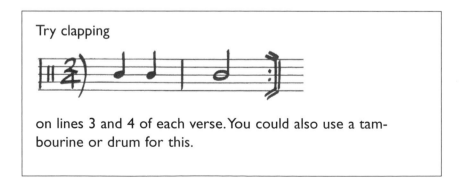

on lines 3 and 4 of each verse. You could also use a tambourine or drum for this.

44

Jingle 10: **Dancing Hands**

3. Run now to face a partner,
   Wave your hands high.
   Clasp these hands above your head
   stretch them to the sky.

4. Now clap your partner's hands,
   one, two and three.
   Right hand, left hand, right again,
   busy as can be!

5. Join hands and dance around,
   one, two and three.
   Leave your partner, wave 'goodbye',
   dance around quite free!

Dancing Hands: *Teacher's Notes*

This jingle is to develop rhythmical awareness and competence. Both clapping and clasping happen at the midline of the body and this is good developmental practice for children who find working at the midline or crossing it difficult, especially if two hands have to do different things. This kind of activity develops laterality and hand dominance.

The hands 'doing a twirl', means that they should be held as if they were going into a muff and then rolled over one another. This is very difficult and makes a good point for observation if difficulties such as dyspraxia (poor coordination) are suspected.

This jingle could be taken as a round, groups of three children or so clapping out the rhythm one after the other. This gives good listening practice and the repetition lets the children who have difficulty coping with the speed catch up.

Working in twos

In verse 3 the children enjoy the challenge of remembering which hand is which and, of course, facing the partner and using the opposite hand does make it tricky. But if the activity is light-hearted and when the jingle is read out slowly with lots of pauses, then the children enjoy the challenge.

After that, joining two hands in a ring is quite easy although skipping round or slip stepping round holds another set of challenges. The last part is free dancing round the hall, which everyone enjoys!

Jingle 11: **Watch Me, I Can Show!**

Verses 1, 3, 5 and 7 are sung as written.
Verses 2, 4 and 6 may be sung to the more flowing rhythm:

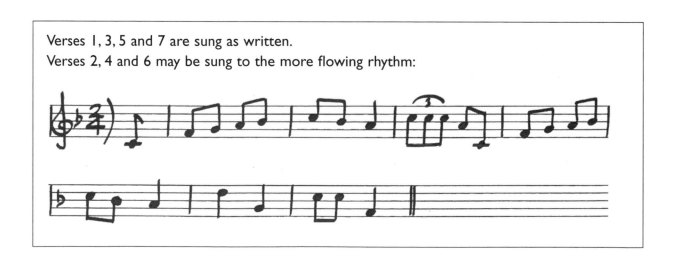

Jingle 11: **Watch Me, I Can Show!**

1. A tiny rabbit scampers past,
   how does he go?
   His bobtail popping up and down.
   Watch me, I can show!

2. A great long snake, he slithers past,
   how does he go?
   He slides around, close to the ground.
   Watch me, I can show!

3. A buzzy bee, he zooms around,
   how does he go?
   He goes here, there and everywhere.
   Watch me, I can show!

4. A kangaroo takes great long leaps,
   how does he go?
   He bounds around, far from the ground.
   Watch me, I can show!

5. A tiny mouse is very quiet,
   how does he go?
   He peeps out, then he darts about.
   Watch me, I can show!

6. A butterfly floats gently past,
   how does he go?
   He swoops and lands so daintily.
   Watch me, I can show!

7. A little child can run so fast,
   till (s)he's aglow,
   Who is that person running there?
   It's (child's name), don't you know?

Watch Me, I Can Show!: *Teacher's Notes*

This jingle lets children understand and demonstrate how animals move. It is a useful way of extending vocabulary if action words such as zoom, slither, bound are tried out.

There is lots of contrast in the kinds of movements animals do and the children could discuss the unusual ways animals move and the speeds at which they travel. A good example would be the sidewinder, a snake which travels at great speeds through the desert moving sideways rather than forwards!

Looking at creatures' bodies against the kind of terrain they live in leads to useful general knowledge, e.g. dolphins and their streamlining, or seagulls with their huge wing-spans which allow them to travel long distances and hover (balance) above the waves.

Sitting in a circle children could take turns to demonstrate the movement of one animal while the others guess what it is. If they can't, the child has to give a verbal clue, e.g. it runs very fast, or has a bobtail, or is very timid.

Once the correct identification has been made, all the children can try.

Jingle 12: **Rainy Days**

LET'S WATCH THE RAIN-DROPS ON THE WINDOW PANE
WHY DO THEY TRIC-KLE DOWN AND NOT GO UP A-GAIN.

Try using a rain-maker for the 1st and 3rd lines of each verse and Indian bells or triangle for the 2nd and 4th lines, using this rhythm:

Jingle 12: **Rainy Days**

1. Let's watch the raindrops
    on the window pane.
    Why do they trickle down
    and not go up again?

2. Where do they come from?
    Look up to the sky.
    There you'll see some puffy clouds
    as they pass slowly by.

3. If they are racing
    speeding past the sun,
    it will be windy, and
    before the day is done.

4. If clouds are soft and white,
    and with flecks of grey,
    it is quite likely that
    we'll have a sunny day!

Rainy Days: *Teacher's Notes*

This is one for quiet contemplation when it's raining and the children can't get outside to play. It is a useful one when the classroom theme is 'The Weather'.

Discussion points

*   How can one tell what the weather is going to be?
*   Do we need television reports?
*   What happened before television – old people's tales about rheumatics!
*   What kinds of jobs are affected by the weather? E.g. fishermen, rescue teams in the mountains, gardeners, builders and farmers.
*   What clothes are suitable for different kinds of weather – and why?

Classroom collage

Making a weather collage can produce an impressive wall display – clouds of cotton wool, rain made out of silver stranded paper, sunshine, sun specs, and brollies outside in to show windy weather.

Fine motor skills

These can be helped by having the children move their fingers down an imaginary window to copy the rain patterns – rather like 'Incy Wincy Spider'!

Jingle 13: **The Clown**

Jingle 13: **The Clown**

1. I'm in the circus,
   jolly and bright.
   My trousers are baggy,
   I look such a fright.
   Hooray, Hooray, Hooray, Ha.

2. I juggle three balls,
   all in the air.
   I'm smiling and happy
   with bright orange hair.
   Hooray, Hooray, Hooray, Ha.

3. Come to my circus,
   dance round the ring.
   Climb in the trapeze,
   where acrobats swing.
   Hooray, Hooray, Hooray, Ha.

4. Gallop like horses,
   grab on the rein,
   It's great fun this circus,
   we'll come back again.
   Hooray, Hooray, Hooray, Ha.

The Clown: *Teacher's Notes*

In this jingle the children should enjoy role play and, as they do, they can act out a storyline – either this one or one they have made up themselves.

Dressing up

This is always good fun. The children love trying to walk with huge shoes or baggy trousers and having their hair in a mess!

There are also skills for them to try – juggling using airflow balls, swinging (a suspended rope in the playground, with adult supervision at all times).

Galloping like the circus horses is good fun and lets teachers see who can manage the galloping action (easier than skipping because the same foot stays in front).

The children can take different circus roles and act them out and learn some of the descriptive words as they do.

- ringmaster – proud, bossy
- trapeze artist – fearless, like a ballet dancer
- clown – funny, comical, loud, colourful, oversized
- juggler – clever, quick, skilful
- acrobats – agile, fearless, good sense of balance
- strong men – muscley, tough.

Discussion points

- How would you like to live in a circus?
- Which part would you like to play?
- Would you have animals in your circus? If so, why; if not why not?
- What kinds of animals?
- Where should circuses be held? Talk about access, i.e. easy to get to, loud noise late at night, safety if animals are caged near houses.
- What about children who live in the circus? Should they have to work there? What sorts of jobs could they do?
- What could be done to make the children welcome in our school?

A circus story

The circus is coming to town. The children form a parade showing off the different costumes they have made. Some hold banners which they have made after discussing what kind of information should be displayed. The parade marches through the town to the field where the circus is to be held.

The first job is to erect the big top and so the strong men heave the ropes while the others form the tent and are pulled open as the men heave. Once the ring is ready, the children in twos become the horses and gallop round (ropes over shoulders and under arms to form reins). They keep evenly spaced as they gallop (teaching awareness of others).

Once this turn is over, the acrobats come on and show what they can do (running and jumping and turning; some children will choose to do cartwheels or handstands) and then the jugglers have their turn.

When this is going on, word comes that the lion has escaped and there is panic (the children run backwards and forwards telling each other 'The lion is out!'). But then the strong men lift a huge net and throw it over the lion. All is well – the lion is led back to his cage and the circus begins again, finishing with a parade leading out of the town. The parade leaders can use percussion: cymbals are especially popular!

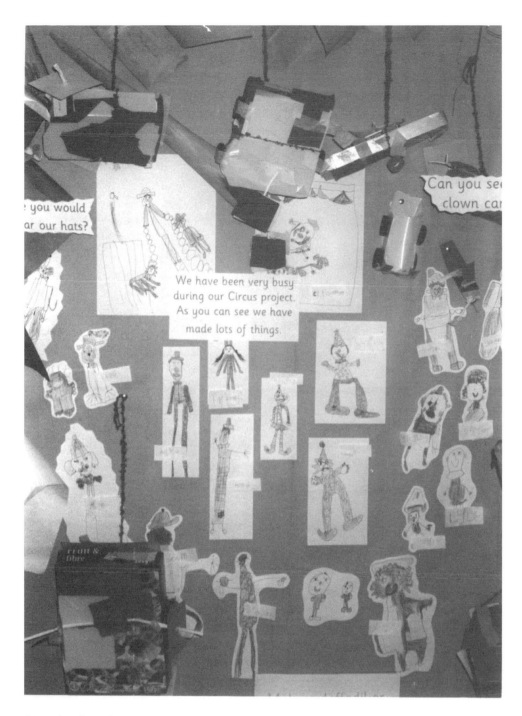

Photo 4a: Clown drawings.

Photo 4b: The clown — learning about symmetry.

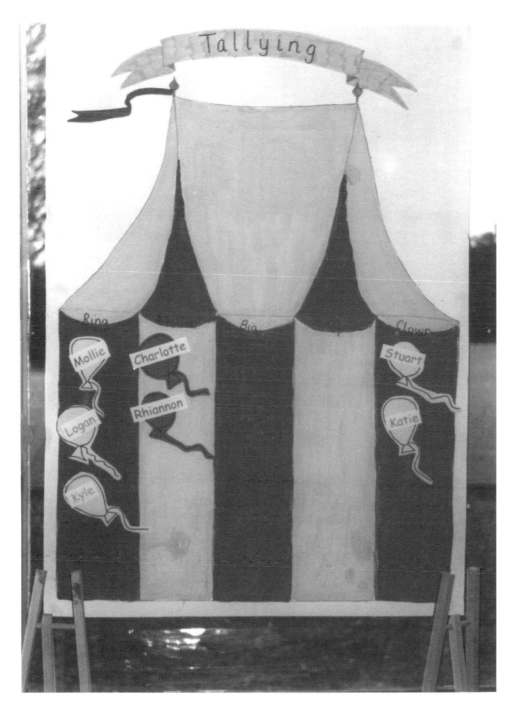

Photo 4b: The clown – early mathematics on a circus theme.

Jingle 14: **The Puppet**

1. I'm a small wooden puppet
   all tied up with string.
   I lie in my box
   only able to sing.

2. It's so sad I can't dance
   for I'd love to be free.
   But elbows and knees
   are tied up you see.

3. Now I'm pulling that string
   and I'll toss it away,
   and now I shall dance
   all the hours of the day!

4. But what is that noise,
   that sound that I hear?
   It's calling me back
   to my wee box, I fear.

5. So I crumple right down
   and tuck elbows in tight,
   and have a wee sleep,
   shut my eyes, say 'Goodnight!'

The Puppet: *Teacher's Notes*

This lesson focuses on developing body awareness and gross motor skills, particularly showing the contrast between moving jerkily with awareness of elbows and knees and dancing smoothly and freely once the strings have been removed. The story is self-explanatory but there is new language to describe the movements, e.g. crumple – what do the children think that means? Can they show? Perhaps they can try crumpling paper to give a visual aid before they try to do it with their bodies? Tossing – how is that different from throwing? Can they look sad and move in a sad way and show a real contrast by dancing happily when they are free?

Discussion

The teacher should have a picture of a puppet or a real one. This allows the jerky movements to be explained. Different kinds of puppets, e.g. glove, string, finger and whole arm puppets like Punch and Judy and marionettes can be discussed, and stories such as Pinocchio are always enjoyed. Some towns, e.g. Biggar in Scotland, have permanent puppet theatres which provide a lovely show for the children.

The children in twos can be the puppet and the puppeteer – this encourages working together and being aware of what the other is doing.

The children need to listen hard so that they change the kind of action they do as the rhyme changes.

Jingle 15: **The Spider**

1. There's a great big spider in my bath
   he's round and very fat.
   He needs eight legs to carry him
   What do you think of that?

2. He has two beady little eyes
   that I can hardly see.
   But when I try to pick him up
   I know that he sees me!

3. He scuttles off – he runs so fast
   or rolls into a ball.
   What else do big fat spiders do?
   They seem no use at all!

4. But if you see the webs they weave
   then suddenly you know
   how clever spiders really are.
   Let's make some webs to show!

The Spider: *Teacher's Notes*

There are other jingles to accompany this one – especially 'Incy Wincy Spider'. The children enjoy making their fingers move rapidly – scuttling – and this is good practice for making them aware of their hands and for practising fine motor skills.

Activity

The main activity is to make spiders, which are easily constructed from old black tights, cotton wool and pipe cleaners. The little ones learn to count up to eight as they prepare the legs and the older ones can make a stunning collage, with glitter covering strands of paper on a black background (see Photo 5).

Lots of input on insects is appropriate – the different kinds, where they live, what they eat, and what they do in the food chain are all fascinating pieces of information for young children. Hopefully, they will appreciate the delicate creatures – looking at the patterns on butterflies and moths can help children appreciate just how beautiful they are.

Photo 5: The spider – glittering collage.

Photo 6: The spider – classroom display. The children sequenced the story of Incy Wincy Spider.

Jingle 16: **Sensations**

1. Smoothly, smoothly stroke a tiny kitten,
   softly, softly, hardly touch its fur.
   Gently, gently, you don't want to be bitten.
   Listen to it purr!

2. Jaggy, jaggy, running on the sand now,
   prickly, prickly, these little stones do cling.
   Razor shells with lots of raggy edges,
   no wonder that they sting!

3. Stiffly, stiffly, march around the room now,
   make your arms and legs stay straight.
   Salute your friend as you march right past now,
   'Halt' means stop and wait!

4. Softly, softly, it's time to go to bed now,
   cuddle down, you'll soon be nice and warm.
   Dream a dream and have a little sleep now,
   safe from any harm!

Sensations: *Teacher's Notes*

Recognition of textures is part of the early years science curriculum. The children who made the collage in Photo 7 collected items and classified them according to their texture and were delighted by the admiration the collage received. Handling the different materials helps tactile awareness and lets children see the effect their actions have on the different ones. In this way they learn to control the strength in their fingers – handling an egg shell or cotton wool being a very different experience from rolling clay or feeling smooth stones.

The jingle brings in experiences the children are likely to have had or ones they can imagine, e.g. running barefoot on the sand. Thinking about stroking a kitten can stimulate discussions on the responsibility involved in keeping pets, while recognising that the kitten's tiny teeth can be razor sharp can stimulate a discussion about their own teeth and how second ones come in, just as they do for the kitten.

Activity

Guessing objects in a feely bag is a favourite activity. As well as enjoying the surprise, the game helps tactile recognition of objects. If some can have a sound as well, e.g. a cat's furry ball with a bell in the centre, then the children are encouraged to use all their senses to investigate.

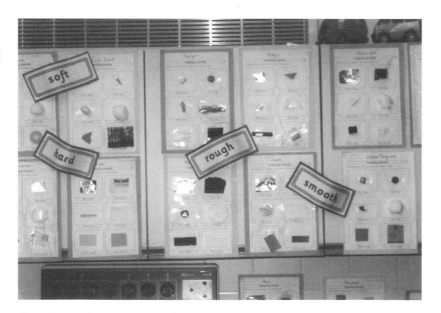

Photo 7: Sensations – classroom display.